Poems on
the Way to
Waking Up

NO RETREAT

Poems on
the Way to
Waking Up

No Retreat

SHAMBHAVI SARASVATI

Jaya Kula Press

110 Marginal Way, #196
Portland, Maine 04101
jayakula.org

© 2016 by Shambhavi Sarasvati
All rights reserved. No part of this book may be reproduced in any form, or by any means, without permission in writing from the publisher.

Cover and interior design and layout: Cecilia Sorochin, Sorodesign
Cover photo by Shambhavi Sarasvati
Back cover photo by Nandikesha Jungwirth

Library of Congress Control Number: 2016906260
Sarasvati, Shambhavi
No Retreat: poems on the way to waking up
ISBN:
978-0-9841634-6-5
0-9841634-6-8

Printed in the United States of America on acid-free paper.

THIS BOOK IS A PRAYER FOR EVERYONE.

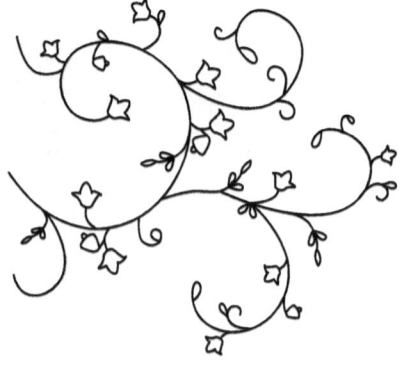

CONTENTS

OPENING	*9*
RETREAT	*11*
GURU	*33*
WISDOM NATURE	*53*
ADVICE	*77*
NO RETREAT	*101*

OPENING

  Most of these poems were written while on spiritual retreat, or during times of the eruption of intense spiritual feeling. They span more than fifteen years of practice.

  I have now and again read a few poems to my students, or circulated them privately. But human beings, even from diverse traditions, encounter similar experiences on the way to waking up. So I have taken the bold step of publishing them. May they be of benefit.

        SHAMBHAVI SARASVATI

        A fire monkey in 2016, the year of the fire monkey

        Portland, Maine

RETREAT

1

I feel tired today.
So many
revelations came
in the night.
Am I hearty enough
for this thing
called Self-
realization?

2

My teacher speaks
her name in dreams.
In contemplation, she says,
Don't be stuck on names!
She is swift in judgment,
more patient than the slowest-growing tree.
I stumble along
and sometimes wonder what she
sees in me.
My own Self,
she says.
And the unstoppable desire
to realize *that*
is you, too?
Very good, she
says.
But I am also the stumbling.
Don't forget.

3

I got so scared
at that new fruition,
I drank a saké
and turned the radio on loud
just to slow down
the unfolding.

Today I find
the wisdom beings
have not abandoned
their woozy shipmate.
I can try again!
Is everyone else
more heroic than I am?

4

My teacher uses
scare tactics
to stop me from
rushing ahead and
following my old
rebellious ways.
This is a joke
between us.
But still, I need her
to do that.

5

When I hear the whine
of freeway tires,
I imagine it's like
the roar one hears
while crossing
the bardos of death.

So I practice relaxing
the six gates
and remaining
undistracted from
my Guru's face.

If I call my Guru's name
while I'm dreaming asleep,
I'm thankful for this sign
that I might also call to her
while dying.

Judging by appearances,
I'm pretty sure this was not
a consciously chosen birth.
I may have been drunk.
If not with alcohol,
certainly with ambition
and greed.

But in this life
at least I have learned
I need help.
And I practice to
remember that.

6

No more
Mahasiddhas
Lamas
Devis
Gurus
Dakinis
holy cows
talking dogs
Buddhas
babies offering
preternatural
transmissions
mind explosions
healers or helpful demons
visit me in
dreams.

She sent them all away
for the sake of
listening.

7

Most Glorious Teacher,
please break down
the rock of my defenses.
Use a sledgehammer!
If these words are insincere,
do it anyway.

8

Eyes are symbols of seeing,
ears of hearing,
skin of touching,
nose of scenting.
The skull is a symbol
of separative mind.

If I embodied more of
this wisdom,
I could travel anywhere
without moving.

9

Before, I amazed myself
at how far I had come.
Now I cry because I am nowhere
near after all this.
I redouble my efforts, or
break off.
It doesn't matter.
The longing is the same.

10

I bow to Saturn,
keeper of records
and doubt.
Without your
cruel eyes,
I would have tried
to suffer less,
clinging to my rock of
certainty, the one stuck
in the middle
of the stream.

11

If you won't respond,
perhaps I should not have spoken.
Whenever I catch
a glimpse of God
that play
of spaciousness,
that sweet breath,
I'm like a pet dog left home
alone too long.
I hear footsteps
on the walk.
I hurl myself against the door
howling and shivering.
Then the footsteps fade,
leaving only the
neighbor's annoyance
at the one who made
all that noise.

12

"Be simple," my
teacher said.
But I didn't listen.
I went off
stalking
the extraordinary.

Ten days now, and
the world's body
hasn't stopped
appearing as sound.
Chanting coming from
everywhere, around the clock.
One night, even eyelids
blinking OM OM OM.

I will be so happy
returning to the world
of clucking chickens,
silent marigolds,
wet porches and
shimmering pine.

An ordinary word with
a neighbor is good medicine.
All I want is to remain
awake in Mothers' clear
and effortless embrace.

Learning this lesson
has been hard
for me.

No wonder the three
gates of human
body, speech and mind,
are the envy of all the realms.

13

There's no point
consulting books
when the answers
live in
earth water
fire air and space,
in world speaking
me listening.
But still I
keep asking:
Why do I understand
so much less than
that?

14

When Masters talk about emptiness,
they mean the experience of realizing
the same always comes and goes.

When Masters say "nothing happens,"
they mean all life
rests in itself.

When Masters mention Great Time,
This is not present,
future or past.

Resting between my awareness
and the awareness of
my teacher,
I have to forget about
disciple and Guru.
I have to forget about naming
and making distinctions.
The middle absorbs these
like snow falling
on a pristine field of snow.

Then suddenly I find
I don't want to Self-realize.
We humans follow the Dharma,
fall in love with our teachers, our
explanations and a feeling of
"not yet there."
Attachment is also to these.
I don't want to let go!

I'm a little ashamed,
and I laugh at myself, too.
A lifetime of
nothing but grace.
This fear is only of
a less familiar known.

15

Sometimes I get sick of this
human vision.
The dharmadhatu
shines through all.
The full moon tantalizes
even through dense fog.

Last night,
I dreamt I was hired
at an hourly wage
to investigate
someone else's crime.
I walked the streets,
diligently performing
this incomprehensible work
until near dawn.

Finally the shops and bars
closed down.
I tried to phone a hotel.
Are there any beds left? I wanted
to ask.

But a neon sign flashed:
"The phones are jammed."
I was alone
and suddenly free
in the empty street.

As I walked on,
I discovered
a ripe half melon
had been in my hand
the whole time.
Why had I left it so long without
tasting?

I raised the fruit to my mouth.
The pink flesh
glowed with the
street lamp's
reflected light.
The cool juice flooded
my throat,
ending thirst.

16

Like the minor devas,
I ate my favored foods
first.
They lasted nearly until
the final day of retreat.
Then I had to stomach
the karma of
maintaining
preferences.

GURU

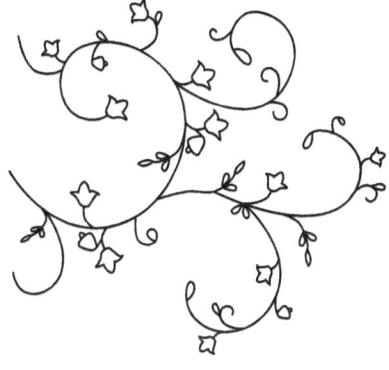

1

First she lured me away
from all other Gurus,
keeping me close,
a young girl tied
to her Mother.

When I grew up a little,
she said,
"Shoo shoo! Your
attachment to me is just
another link in samsara's chain!"
But I didn't want to go!

Then she showed me:
All Gurus are one.
After twenty-five years,
I met my real teacher
for the first time.

2

She is the lightening sky.
Her rays emanate
first bird songs.
She is also the cock's crow and
the coldness creeping skin.
A neighbor turns on
a kitchen light.
That is she.
She is the mantra on my lips
and the one who
gave it to me.

3

I confessed my worst fear:
that *you* might be lonely, too.
So you showed me your one
body of bliss.
Then the skeptic argued—
maybe you're just blissed out!
Who wants that?
So you showed me your
body of wide awake clarity.
But those feel
separate.
What about their
unison?
Dear Mother,
that's when I fell
headlong into
your immeasurable lap.

4

Who knows?
Am I clinging to
them or they to me,
those faded attachments,
nearly forgotten friends and
relations
announcing themselves
in dreams with
too hearty hellos?
One honest moment of
surrender and
Ma sends them off
Her sharp, dancing steps
dazzle the spine,
up and out to meet Herself
at the top, the
infinite stage.

5

I was speaking the language of unconditional love.
She told me what I meant.

I asked what to give.
She said, "your will."

I asked how.
She said, "your longing."

I asked the cost.
She said, "You are *That*."

Finally, after all those
interrogations,
she placed her hand on my heart
and the questioner and the answer became
One.

6

I stand up
beneath her
feet.
The View is
limitless.

Prostrating to
her,
the three worlds
stretch
out.

There is no
horizon
but she.
She has no
horizon.

Everything is
her intelligence.
The room
shines
with it.

For now
she keeps me
close, restrained
from chasing
the merely many.
Her infinity is
the Supreme Mandala
of Protection.

To love her without reserve.
To be her without
hesitation.
This is always
accomplished,
but still
it comes and goes.

7

Loving her,
I have to love
your Guru, too.

There is only one
Teacher.

8

She is my only refuge.
Not thoughts and plans.
Not friends or lineage.
Not deciding this or that.
Not purification.
Not even understanding.

Her presence is the treatment
for distraction.
I turn to her.
Her grace is
the medicine for karma.
I turn to her.
She is Mother,
Father,
Friend,
Bindu
and
Light.

She is the Guru of
infinite means.
Every happenstance,
her grace and her
instruction.

Arrive with
nothing.
That is the hardest task.
Be her
crucible,
her river,
her cup.

Follow only her
and see what happens.

9

Both Limited and Unlimited

A poem about Anandamayi Ma

Ma liked to take big steps
when she walked.
She wore lotus
garlands and laughed
open-mouthed.
She enjoyed everything at
nobody's expense.

Ma slayed egos and
rescued plants.
She chatted in bed
and caused earnest men
to weep with joy.
She danced to divine music,
spoke the rishis' tongue,
and her teeth were stained betel-red.

Ma never slept while she was sleeping.
She was never entranced.
Dakinis showed her other realms and worlds.
Wide awake, she taught her human sisters well.

Ma made no
spiritual quests.
She did not journey
to the body of rainbow lights.

She is the pilgrimage,
and she is the resolution of human life.

Each time,
when that body is done,
a spring of fierce compassion
takes its place.
The source of that spring
is the trident of God,
endlessly
birthing a new
City of Light.

10

The roses offer
themselves to Ma
as they die.
One by one,
the petals drop
at her feet,
and into her lap.

Soon, only the
stem remains.
It is She!
It is He!
The infinite, open way.
Each day,
remember this.

As soon as you can,
relax and let
the petals of
fate and fixation
fall.

Do puja with
these offerings
of Self to Self.
Then see how wondrous She is,
her naked glory shines
in color, silk, and scent.

11

The wordless
exaltation I feel
contemplating Guru
is herself experiencing
herself.

This wonderousing called
Vajra pride
her enjoyment of
her own body:
the world

Once
in a human body
she said,
I have come to inspect
my creatures.
She meant
I have come to inspect
myself.

She knows herself
smells, tastes, sees, touches
herself
through us
also herself.

I woke up today
full full full
and wrote this
by myself
for myself
beside myself.

12

Please don't ask me to be
your ordinary friend.
It's too painful
remaining silent when
I see your enlightened body
poking out
from beneath your sleeves.

Please don't ask me to be
your forever friend.
That's too special
and lonely and anyway,
immortal friendship
is just the devotion
of nature to
itself.

Please stop asking about my mother
and father.
Don't expect me to have brothers
sisters, nephews, aunts or
cousins first or removed.

All relatives are relative and
furthermore,
please remain calm if
I don't fall in love, or
grieve as I used to when
people die or
disappear.

Now, but not in time,
she is my single
Friend.
And only through
her do I meet you,
all you marvelous ones
again.

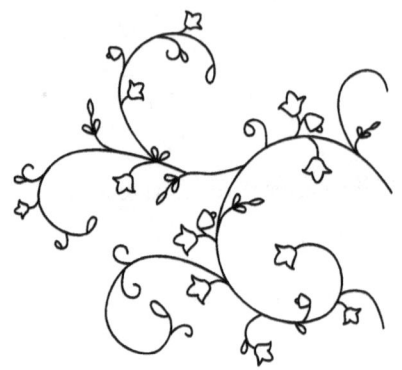

WISDOM NATURE

1

Even in iTunes
a recording
of an old monk singing
Krishna and Arjuna's song
fills the house
with the glory of
Self-awareness.

2

I learned to stop
seducing with "me."
But until now,
I didn't know
the dance that seduces
everyone.

3

Reality cares equally for
those in deepest ignorance.
We live in such
a generous world.

4

The Lord can make
a world with
two colors,
three shapes,
no rivers and
no dinner parties
or tattoos.

A person could spend
lifetimes
unaware of the
capacity for
scent.

A slightly pleasurable,
but also irritating
scratching sensation
could be the only
method of communication
between you and
your world.

God is great.

Time is experienced differently
by the various forms of life.
Once you leave here,
how long will it be
before you once again
light the incense,
ring the bell and
appreciate marigolds
as you sit for your morning
prayers?

5

Yesterday,
I saw a dozen
Buddha faces etched
in branches.
Some had eyes closed,
some eyes open.
All rested in
a state of contemplation.

Today,
peering at trees,
I cannot find
a single Buddha
even when I
try hard
to invent one.

Life writes
messages like this.
Learning to read
reduces the desire for
so many books.

6

Why sleep
in the face of
this shining?

Nights disappoint
passing
in darkness.

The Realized are few,
yet one wants
only to join them and
regain the world.

Pay attention to
ordinary oceans,
sun, moon, fire,
and waves.

Surprising how
appearances speak
so eloquently of
the way things really are.

7

A deer bounded up
to where I sat.
A bit afraid, I
still reached out
to stroke him.
After this, he lay his head
contentedly in my lap.

Later, other
animals came calling—
a jaguar, a monkey,
a dog and I don't know who else.

Everyone cooperated to make
a communal meal.

Human life is
overly dramatic.
I am grateful
for this dream.

8

The tops of my
new leather shoes
are stitched with the face of an animal.
The face is stylized and subtle.
A goat, or a cow or a lizard, perhaps.

In my dreams,
dogs come to play.
We hold telepathic conversations
in dog languages.
Another time,
Krishna's cow offers me a flower
from his own mouth.

I buy meat in the market
and see the lives of animals
before they were killed.
I feel sun on my back
and taste the sweet grass.
Gazing at bones,
I know what it is to walk on four legs
instead of two.

Everywhere, animals
reveal themselves.
The animals are not saying,
"Don't eat me!"
But they want us to know
we are all here together
thinking,
feeling
and dying.

9

A tiger hunts fiercely all day
and loses many prey before eating.
A monkey plays and never falls
from the branch.

Today the monkey followed
the tiger's advice
and behaved stupidly
with someone she respects.
The precise direction
of everything changed.

On another level,
no step can ever be mis-taken.
And no action can be
understood on
the plane of mistakes.
Human beings live
this manifold Reality.

Later, in the kitchen,
the lively girl Rose
sang a spontaneous song:
Shambhavi! Shambhavi!
Ra Ra Ra!
Ra! Dharmakaya
Ra! Sambhogakaya
Ra! Nirmanakaya
This stupendous life!

10

God is making
plastic-coated
base metal
twist ties in
Indiana.

She's appearing
in Bolivia as
deforestation,
reforestation
and all those who
have an opinion
about trees.

God is
a souped-up
hemi, a
soup kitchen,
and in the soup
with unpaid
bills.

God is various
kinds of
unawareness and
infinite paths
to remedy that.

God is Christ.
God is Krishna.
God is Buddha.
God is Shiva.
God is Allah.
God is Coyote.
God is Ma.
God is every scripture
and also every tabloid
magazine.

God is limited and unlimited.
She is neither of
these.

God is the experience of
death and birth,
living and dying.

God is not born and
never passes away.

Every being is
on the road to
God, and there is
no road but God.

If you disagree with me,
God is disagreeing with me.

God is laughing at her own
joke.

God is good.

11

Question from the Kali Yuga

Those sisters who
circumambulated
Shiva's mountain a
hundred times, who
tamed rapists and
thieves with
a word and a look,
who offered
their own kneecaps
to mend a stranger's limp,
who lived in caves or
ran naked, spouting
poetry in the streets
of Srinagar,
who are these sisters to me,
counting beads on my
sunny bench, wondering,
shall I sit for another
hour or two before
bed?

12

A new wren
learning to fly
around the redwood tree
nearly stalls
in mid-air.

Better to stay
here, dear bird,
and hop from leaf
to worm.

Don't fly alone
until Mother comes
to show you
and say "it's time."

13

These flashes of
waking up
are enough to keep me
following
whatever you ask.
I *do* want to live within this
dazzling clarity.

14

Practitioners want to know:
How long will it take
to send off the
showy monkeys,
stalking tigers and
hibernating bears?
And what about those
dreamy llamas, mistaking
themselves for the real thing?

Here's the truth:
The apprenticeship to
your own Self lasts
longer than anything
you'll find in this one life.

15

Meeting with a Dakini

Dakinis are female wisdom beings whose function is to transmit teachings into the human realm.

Beautiful sister,

world shaper,

dakini lover,

my enjoyments are all

laid at your feet

because they are born at your feet.

And then, from the crystal point

of your one true eye

All sky

All cloud

All moisture

All smoothness

All breeze

All space

All youth

All play

All jokes

All elegance

All innocence

All clarity

All skill

All instruction

All warnings

All wisdom

All nakedness

All kisses

All compassion

All quiet joy.

Kind sister, your supple lightening makes
all bodies dance.
Please help me remember
the One Time when we two first met.

16

Dakinis dance
on mandalas of sound and light.
A foot placed just so
at junctures of rays
gives entrance
to various dimensions,
and with mudras
they control the directions.
This is the elegant travel method of dakinis.

We call dakinis "skydancers"
and imagine they glide
cloudlike and serene
through uninterrupted blue.
We don't perceive
the elegant and precise steps of dakinis,
tracing subtle mandalas that ride
primordial swells
of space and time

Here on earth,
compassionate dakinis
teach those of more condensed light
our versions of the dance.
With their sisterly aid,
we explore the human dimension
while dancing in our leather shoes
on mandalas of plastic,
wood and paint

We shout in celebration
having barely learned to emulate
the elegant gestures
of dakinis.
Or we cry,
sensing the mandala is both
an invitation and a pledge.
One day, wide awake,
we will join this
interdimensional dance,
this shared life.

ADVICE

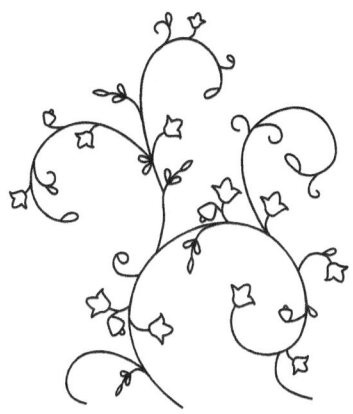

1

Sit with sincerity
at the feet
of an unrealized teacher,
and eventually
you will learn to sit
at everyone's feet.

Sit with devotion
at the feet
of a realized Master,
and eventually
you will understand
the sense in which
everyone is realized.

Meet, even briefly,
a human being
abiding in the one taste
of realization and nonrealization,

and you will keep
company with a world
devoted to itself
without exception
and without alteration.

2

Teachers
move around
so students can realize
there is no coming
and no going.

Follow kirtan
and adapt to a
moving landscape
of pitch
and modulation.

Follow your teacher
and discover the ocean
that hosts all currents and seasons.

If you long to hold back
life's incessant
becoming,
experience *that*
in the mirror
of your teacher's traveling.

If you long to
relax in
your teacher's
presence,
realize *that* as
wisdom
ever arising.

2

When the fire rages,
lie down close to the ground.
That's where you'll find
the refuge of
space and breath.

I have seen those
who were demons
take human form
and bend in sincere
devotion to kiss
the hands of their
teachers.

I have seen
copper-realm beings
sing the names of
God and make
small offerings that would disgrace
you or me,
but in their hands
are magnificent.

Devotion is the
medicine for
the illness of
feeling tricked and
unloved.

Practicing humility is
the medicine for
the abject.

Following without question
is the medicine
for ignorance
that tortures with
skepticism and rage.

Company is the
medicine for
loneliness that
leads us to reject
company.

Please listen carefully.
Our world is just like this.

If you feel small,
get as low as you can and practice
a larger smallness.
Ask for help.
Accept it in any form.
Don't interfere
with the ways of the world,
and you will slowly discover
there is nothing
wrong.

3

Despite the preachers,
never criticize yourself
or others
on account of desire.

The most hated desire
is nothing but divinity
seeking its
inevitable return.

At the feet of the one
who opens the gates,
make an offering
of your weak cravings.

Then with warrior longing
let wisdom sweep you toward
the all-encompassing
dimension.

4

The minor Gods live
attached to
their portion of
minor God bliss.

Their deaths are
full of pain.

My teachers warned me
not to die
in one of those
bliss realms.

Stay awake!
Take your knocks as you go.
Don't cling to
half-baked ideas
of samsara and nirvana.

People long
to feel happy.
They hide out
in concepts,
spouting teachings
to avoid the sting of
being taught.

It's easy to
convince others
you have realized
a wider View.

If your Oneness
is disturbed by
personalities,
if you always have
unbeatable transcendental explanations for
XYZ,
if you no longer recognize
your own suffering,
pinch yourself!
Hard!

Or if this doesn't work,
pray for a teacher
who will pinch you
much harder than that.

5

With all those theories
you've been cooking lately,
you might as well
say "Three Musketeers and
Rin Tin Tin."

That's how much sense
you're making.

Why not say "ocean?"
Why not say "salt?"
Why not say "moon?"
Why not say "blue?"
Why not say "love?"
Why not say "yes?"
Why not say "Let's go?"
Now you're talking!

The complexities
you enjoy are wisps of
echoes.
Follow your longing,
then God's enjoyment of
infinity will be
your own.

Open your arms,
leap into her
vast embrace.
What you call
intelligence, what is it
compared to this?

6

An old book advises:
Stare at a flower
for fifteen minutes,
and you will enter into
God consciousness.

Century after century,
philosophers keep trying
to define beauty.
But beauty always escapes
the prison of
words.

This is why staring at
a beautiful flower
can cause some discomfort.
We become anxious when
Reality runs out ahead.

We glance at flowers,

turning them into decoration.

But if you relax

while meditating on a flower,

you will discover

the infinite,

eternal life.

7

Because you are
God becoming God,
all commitments are naturally fulfilled.
The intricate weave
of everything-at-once
pulls a golden thread
and you are off!
The only authentic vows
are those
that take us,
not the vows we take.

When a vow comes for you,
keep your eyes open,
and your body relaxed.

Be like a newborn baby
tossed into space,
curious and soft
no matter what.

More than artificial vows,

we need this bravery

and to remember

our natural talent

for being swept away.

8

Walk with your mind married
to the bottoms of your feet.
Feel the ground, the floor.
Feel its texture, temperature and slant.
Feel your feet straighten and bend,
come and go.

Your feet carry the weight of a great
wisdom:
that you are an ordinary being
in an ordinary world.
Walking and wandering,
you will never arrive
until you understand
this.

When you stray
into fantasies of accomplishment
or discontent,

just become aware
of the bottoms of your feet
and live there, as the world
moves inevitably on its
roundabout course.
This way of walking is good medicine
for the illness of bothering to be
anything but yourself.

9

Every passage has its
disasters.
A wise yogini told me:
When you want to help
sentient beings,
you will encounter obstacles.

The great ones
have met accidents,
illness,
failure and loss.
But suffering
isn't the sign of greatness
we had been hoping for.

Yogis are not martyrs.
We just try to remain
relaxed and use
skillful means
to protect our practice,
no matter what
happens, or doesn't.

10

Dear students,
I never stopped
doing practice
since the day I
was first named.
This is the only
Tantrik secret
I know.

Dear students,
I worked hard
to recognize my
teachers as my
enlightened Self.
This is the only
yoga I know.

Dear students,
I looked straight at
myself, not
running away

even when others
rejected what they
saw in me.
This is the only
courage I know.

Dear students,
when I discovered
true Guru,
I lay at
her feet while
she rained down
blows.
This is the only
mercy I know.

Dear students,
Guru is amazement!
Teachings are amazement!
Aliveness is nothing but
amazement!
You can get here by walking.
And that is amazement, too.

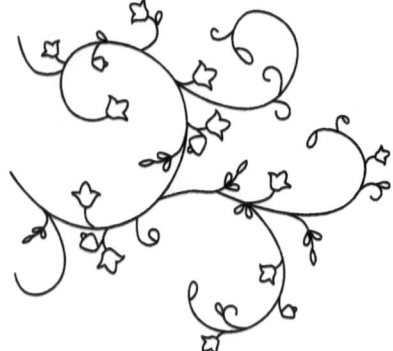

NO RETREAT

1

Let's go stay in a ruined place
where the worst has come and gone.

Let's live where there is no hope of
those former lives returning.

Let's sit in the evidence of apocalypse
where everyone's worst fears have come to pass.
There won't be anything left to guard against
and nothing to clasp.

Come walk with me where the city has tumbled down
and the grandeur is in the wreckage
of what we had built.

Let's rest together in the quiet that follows destruction,
dance a little,
sing some.

2

I felt sad,
coming across
one of my old names.
Then I remembered,
Shambhavi!
You have every name.
I enjoyed both of
these moments—
the first one
watery and
warm,
the second with
neither flavor nor
temperature.

3

Real love is the
solvent that dissolves
exclusive ties to
all our beloveds—
family, enemies, parents and friends,
and even to our teachers
and the devas.
Purna Brahma Narayani means
complete equality in all worlds.

Hearing this, most
people are not interested.
It even terrifies
those who decide
not to run away.

The trick is
to keep surrendering
and try to develop
confidence in
the Return

.

4

There is no nakedness
like stillness.
If I came for something
it might be this.

5

There would be a book about love,
and every word would be given
without any restraint.
And those who lived their days
reading the book,
would become *that*.

Or there would be a glance
from which reality poured
without any restraint.
And whoever passed
through the boundless
stream of this glance
would become *that*.

Then, there would be a touch
from whose smallest surface
the world gives itself
without any restraint.
And whoever held themselves steady
under this touch
would be everywhere held by *that*.

Or there would be a sound,
playing day and night
without any restraint.
If my skin became
an unbroken instrument
for this sound,
I would play like *that*.

And there would be a Friend,
in whose company none would suffer
any restraint.
And the friend of that Friend
would live in a state of grace
and continually become That.

6

Magnificent is the mother of form.
Magnificent is the mother of no form.
Life is magnificence.

Tender is the mother who answers our call.
Tender is the mother who wields the knife.
Life is tenderness.

Emptiness is the daughter
who opens the door
to openness,
the mother
of all.

Openness is the
luminous lap.
Beyond mother and father.
Beyond Shiva and Shakti.
Not beyond
this.

You are welcome!
You are welcome!
We are all welcome!

7

Moon Poem for Li Po

I'm no longer praying
the moon will
give way to the sun.

All that hard time trying
to pull down
the night.

I'm stopping all of it.

If my teachers beat me,
I'll flop around.

For now I only want to do
the pure Buddha practice
and relax.

Who wants to die
chasing the moon?

8

Sometimes this life
is over-the-top
spectacular.
Other times
I can't stand
the poverty of
myself.

Human beings
sound like
every key on
an infinite piano.
It's a matter of
how many notes
you can reach
and play.

9

Certain Sannyas

Mastered by clarity,
my childhood died
and all my family relations.
The phantom cord
burned and offered
to the One with
infinite stories, but no imaginings.

A sickness arrived.
After two days, it recognized itself as grief.
Still, the Lively One's grace
surged through
day and night.

Everyone drank
from God's flooding cup.
Only the pain of surrender
makes possible such sharing.

Night brought dreams of houses.

The inhabitants gone.

Thieves vanquished.

The rooms sealed,

emptied of time and even

nostalgia.

From painful absence to learning

there is none.

Abandoned to find there is no abandoning.

Awe and devotion

continually arising.

Because of your part in this,

ancestors and relations,

I thank you. I thank you all.

10

No longer outraged,
naturally outrageous,
playing with you
is the tenderest
game.

Listen up!
I take myself funseriously.
Same to all of you!

Enjoying
without condition,
no holds barred.
Your real nature is a jewel,
indestructible within
shining appearances.

11

May your name be always on my lips,
whether speaking or silent,
whether in conversation
or prayer.

Every word I say is telling about you.
Every ordinary pause, and the living expanse.
May I never forget this though
having forgotten, it remains true.

Beyond sound or no sound,
memory or forgetting,
the heart swells over full
and all day and night,
you never do anything, Lord
but flow out.

About Jaya Kula Press

Jaya Kula Press is a project of Jaya Kula, a registered 501(c)3 nonprofit organization headquartered in Portland, Maine.

Jaya Kula Press supports dharma practitioners by presenting spiritual teachings that are precise, practical, faithful to their origins and yet accessible to a wide range of people. We currently publish the teachings of Shambhavi Sarasvati, the spiritual director of Jaya Kula.

About Jaya Kula

Jaya Kula is a vibrant, nonprofit householder community offering opportunities to learn and practice in the direct realization traditions of Trika Shaivism and Dzogchen. Our main centers are in Portland: Maine and Oregon.

Mailing Address:
110 Marginal Way, #196
Portland, ME 04101
USA

Email: sayhi@jayakula.org
Phone: (207)358-0121
Website: jayakula.org

Jaya Kula Press Titles
By Shambhavi Sarasvati

Pilgrims to Openness: direct realization Tantra in everyday life - 2009

Tantra: the play of awakening - 2012

Returning: exhortations, advice and encouragement from the heart of direct realization practice - 2015

No Retreat: poems on the way to waking up - 2016

Nine Poisons, Nine Medicines, Nine Fruits - forthcoming 2016

The Reality Sutras – forthcoming 2017

www.ingramcontent.com/pod-product-compliance
Lightning Source LLC
Chambersburg PA
CBHW020658300426
44112CB00007B/432